The Little Business Book With
BIG IDEAS

The Little Business Book With
BIG IDEAS

Maxims for Success in Management and Marketing

James Posner
Illustrated by Irwin Perton

iUniverse, Inc.
New York Lincoln Shanghai

The Little Business Book With BIG IDEAS
Maxims for Success in Management and Marketing

iUniverse books may be ordered through booksellers or by contacting:

iUniverse
2021 Pine Lake Road, Suite 100
Lincoln, NE 68512
www.iuniverse.com
1-800-Authors (1-800-288-4677)

Because of the dynamic nature of the Internet, any Web addresses or links contained in this book may have changed since publication and may no longer be valid.

ISBN: 978-0-595-43056-7 (pbk)
ISBN: 978-0-595-87398-2 (ebk)

Printed in the United States of America

Dedication

To all those who have mentored me—especially Herbert Seegal at Macy's and James Reedy at Allied. I hope some of their wisdom, together with my life experiences, will help others in the difficult, rewarding and creative job of management.

Introduction

Over twenty years ago *What They Don't Teach You at Harvard Business School* graced the bestseller list. In 256 pages, the author revealed to readers the lessons for business success.

Now here is the much shorter *The Little Business Book with Big Ideas,* which offers easy-to-grasp, easy-to-remember wisdom. You'll discover sage advice for the business circumstances and life situations that you confront every day.

During the more than thirty years that Jim Posner has been my friend, I have watched him time and time again cut through the confusion of a big concept or idea and condense it into a few very memorable and valuable words. You will see in this book concepts you have heard before and may have forgotten. But with Jim's gift for simplicity and clarity, you will remember them forever.

Robert Gordman
Author
The Must-Have Customer

Preface

I've been lucky—as a young man I was blessed to have two mentors at different times who took an interest in me and thought that I had the potential to be a good top-management executive.

In their turn, they kept their eyes on me as they put me into business situations that were important to them, but, of course, became great learning opportunities for me. Some of these were big league situations. They served as turning points in my career in management.

Everyone should be so lucky.

Now, after more than thirty years in top management, I realize that the principles I learned were so immutable and constant, they could be applied to every business situation.

They have become known as "JP-isms."

For a time, I compiled them for myself, but friends and associates encouraged me to publish them.

I have put each idea into an easy-to-remember format and accompanied it with a breezy illustration by Irwin Perton—no long chapters, no long explanations.

Use them. They will work for you. They are time tested.

JP

The Little Business Book
With BIG IDEAS

A carpenter
can cut only the
length of the wood.

*Always calculate the dimensions of
your task and know that you
can't exceed them.
4 ÷ 5 doesn't work!*

In any plan, look for the FF— the Fatal Flaw.

There is always one. It could be time, money, people, concept. Find it!

Analysis Paralysis

You have to know when to stop.
Don't get lost in the paperwork.
It's not "want to know,"
but "need to know."

Bad News is usually followed by more Bad News.

In business, problems don't get fixed quickly. "Negatives" need to be dealt with before "positives" emerge.

Come down
hard on the sin,
not the sinner.

Separate the people from the deed.
When you start personalizing,
people recoil or attack.
Punish the sin; spare the sinner.

Competence builds Confidence ... Confidence builds Competence.

This unending cycle
continues from wherever you start.

Customers are not computers.

No matter what messages you send, customers remember only what affects them personally.

Delegation and Abdication are not the same and should not be confused.

Responsibilities must be clearly defined.

Dog bite
or Snake bite?
Know the difference.

*A dog bite hurts only for a few days,
but a snake bite can kill you.
Always know which one
you are dealing with.*

Don't get drunk on your own liquor.

The temptation to love your own ideas is great ... but make very sure to be objective.

Don't invite the camels under your tent; they will "dump" on you.

Know who your enemies are; don't get too friendly with your competitors.

Don't throw away the picture if only the frame is cracked.

Concentrate on the big picture.
Don't let the little things throw you off.

Don't use a cannon to shoot a sparrow.

Articulate the objectives
before you launch a project.

Dual responsibility is NO responsibility.
When everyone is in charge, no one is in charge.

Only single, clear responsibilities produce the best results.

Expenditures always rise to meet income.

True at any level ... corporate and personal.

Expect the Unexpected.

It always happens.
You can't escape it.
Be prepared!

In Marketing anything, frequency is more important than reach.

It's better to reach 1,000 people ten times than 10,000 people once.

Marketing Truth: in niches there are riches.

In this huge country, you can get rich with a very small market share.

"Cheap" rent has killed more people than bullets.

Be wary when something appears too good to be true. It probably is.

Measure twice ...
Cut once.

*Never make impulsive decisions
about important matters.*

One Robin doesn't make a spring.

Be very careful with fragmentary information.

Planning is a never-ending process.

Planning is not to be confused with a book of plans. Planning is dynamic and continuing; making a book of plans is static.

Ready ... Fire ... Aim!
is much more effective than
Ready ... Aim ... Fire!

Don't delay moving forward.
It's better to take action and
make corrections along the way.

Sales in the register are the same as ballots in the voting box.

Your customers are always voting.

The Committee
always picks beige.

Group consensus tends to pick the middle ground, which is not necessarily the most efficient or best choice.

Good management must:

- Set the standard
- Communicate the standard
- Enforce the standard

The first place to look for a helping hand is at the end of your arm.

The road to Success is always under construction.

**Two things
necessary
to accomplish
anything:
Mission and Passion.**

The seven P's ... remember them:
    Piss
    Poor
    Planning
    Produces
    Piss
    Poor
    Performances

Unseen is Untold ...
Untold is Unsold.

Customers must be called to action.

You are not lost
if you have
no destination.

*If you don't know where you're going,
any road will take you there.*

**If the Student
hasn't learned,
the Teacher
hasn't taught.**

If you look back at yesterday, you'll trip on tomorrow.

Now is the only thing that counts.

If you want to catch a fish, you have to think like a Fish, not like a Fisherman.

Information is oxygen.

You can't live without it!

In marketing anything, always look for and exploit the DDs: *Demonstrative Differences.*

In the legion of the blind, the one-eyed man is king.

You have to be only a little bit better to succeed.

It's not
Who's right …
it's What's right.

This should appear above the door
of every business everywhere.

You can't take the Profits out if you don't put the Profits in.

Profit should be the **top** line in business. If you make profit, the bottom line is just the residue of what's left.

Profit is the purpose of the enterprise.

You have two ears
and one mouth …
and they should
be used in the
same proportion.

You have to break an egg to make an omelette.

Sometimes you have to take an unpleasant action to get a good result.

You can't buy Pies with Percentages.

You must pay in dollars. Percentages buy nothing. I'm sorry they don't teach this in school; it can kill you.

You have to get them under the tent to sell them the peanuts.

Driving traffic to the business is **the** essential activity in any business that deals with customers.

The trend
is your friend.

Whether it's "up" or "down,"
you have to read it correctly.

"Steak Cheap" is not "Cheap Steak."

The first is a bargain; the other's a disappointment.

Pioneering doesn't pay—it's not important to be "first."

Being a close second after something is proven pays off better and is much less expensive.

**Facts are friends—
your best friends
are truths.**

Trees and companies die from the top.

978-0-595-43056-7
0-595-43056-2